5/07

0 00 14 0051650 4

Lovingly dedicated to the
special grandfathers in my life:

Richard Bruce Cowdrick (1908–1979), *I'll never forget when
you pushed my hand in Grandma's sugar bowl.*

George August Seiler (1902–1990), *I'll always remember the
incredible model-train layout you built and reading Curious
George stories together.*

Olav Brunvoll (1900–1980), *How I wish I could have met you.*

Stian Skjaevesland Larsen (1906–2003), *I'm so thankful that
you enthusiastically shared your Norwegian heritage with your
great-grandchildren.*

Published in Nashville, Tennessee, by Thomas Nelson, Inc.

Published in association with William K. Jensen Literary Agency, Eugene, Oregon.

Project Editor: Lisa Stilwell

Designed by Greg Jackson, Thinkpen Design, LLC

ISBN-10: 1-4041-0445-3
ISBN-13: 978-1-4041-0445-7

Printed and bound in the United States of America

ALL MY BAD HABITS

I LEARNED FROM

GRANDPA

LAUREL SEILER BRUNVOLL

THOMAS NELSON
Since 1798

NASHVILLE   DALLAS   MEXICO CITY   RIO DE JANEIRO   BEIJING

Table of Contents

"Sure, have all the candy you want."

"*In every real man a child*
is hidden that wants to play."

FRIEDRICH WILHELM NIETZSCHE

The Last Straw

BY LAUREL SEILER BRUNVOLL

S ee ya soon!" Grandpa yelled and waved from the rolled-down window. The beige Lincoln Town Car backed out of the driveway and turned around. After one jerky movement, his vehicle lurched forward and sped away. Trish, a young mother, cringed as she heard her three sons' loud voices feverishly encouraging Grandpa to drive faster.

She tried not to imagine the actual speed of the car as her dad drove such precious cargo around town and on the highway. She remembered how just last week Ryan told everyone at dinner about stoplights. "Red means stop, green means go, and yellow means go faster," the three-year-old proudly explained.

After exchanging accusatory glances with her husband, they both decided Ryan must have learned this from another frequent family driver...Grandpa.

Shaking off her worries, Trish sat down to enjoy the quiet of the house. Several cups of coffee later, she enjoyed the luxury of reading a novel in solitary surroundings. It didn't take her long to become completely involved in the action story.

Suddenly, she looked at the clock and quickly put down her book. *Wow, where did the time go? They'll be back any minute.*

Hurrying to get the table set, Trish filled everyone's glasses with ice water. Even though her dad had promised to bring back a fast-food dinner for the whole family, she felt less guilty if she used regular dishes and silverware. *At least I put together a fruit salad*, she thought.

Several car doors slammed. Within seconds, all three boys bounded into the kitchen. Grandpa wasn't far behind. Excitement and laughter covered their faces—along with evidence of chocolate ice cream.

I guess their dinner has been ruined, Trish thought. But she knew they had had a good time and decided against chiding her dad about giving them ice cream before dinner again.

"Thanks for bringing dinner, Dad," said Trish. "It smells delicious."

"No problem! Thanks for letting me have the boys this afternoon," he said with a little chuckle. "We had a lot of fun."

A meal of greasy fried chicken, hot biscuits, mashed potatoes, and gravy was a family favorite. Within minutes and all at once, the boys tried to tell their mom about their outing.

While everyone else was talking, Ryan picked up one of the straws from the restaurant and carefully pulled the paper off one end. His small fingers lifted the straw to his mouth. One great big breath and a quick blow and the white paper was off. It rocketed toward the ceiling and then gently floated down to the floor.

"Look what I can do!" he shouted.

Before Trish could say anything, Mark grabbed his straw and took dead aim. The paper hit Ryan right in the middle of his forehead. Then it fell to the floor too.

"Hey!" Ryan shouted again. "Stop it!"

Ryan grabbed another straw from the pile. This time his angry blow caused the paper to sail sideways and then up. Because of the angled flight, it somehow lodged on the inner part of the chandelier.

Grandpa glanced up with a smirk and then quietly picked up a straw. His straight aim shot directly across the table and smack dab into Mark's cheek. Mark whipped around. "I'm going to get you, Jimmy!"

Jimmy gave him a confused look. Mark turned to face him with his paperless straw. Compensating, he made a tiny ball from a piece of napkin and loaded it into the barrel of his straw. Grandpa watched and tried to hide his merriment, but he wasn't successful.

"Okay, that's enough," Trish said.

"But Grandpa did it!" said Jimmy, the five-year-old. "He showed us at the ice cream place."

"Yeah, and his paper landed in some lady's food," laughed Mark, who was seven.

"What?"

"The people sitting behind us. It landed on her plate," Mark continued.

Trish, now completely horrified, closed her eyes just for a second as she pictured the four of them at Friendly's Restaurant...

The boys talked excitedly about who would win the next World Series and asked for Grandpa's valuable sports opinions. Once that matter was settled, the drinks arrived. And free refills of dark, caffeinated soda kept coming and coming. The waitress cleared old glasses as she brought refills, each with a new glass and a new straw.

Grandpa expertly ripped off the thin white paper covering the end of the straw. With a flick of his wrist, he quickly twisted the opposite end and brought it up to his mouth. "Here! Watch this," he said to all three.

With cheeks puffed and lips pursed, he looked like a trumpet player. Then, taking one big breath, he made that little paper shoot straight up to the ceiling. And down it floated.

The boys turned around in the booth to watch the paper's flight. Slowly, slowly it fell, getting closer and closer to a nearby table. Mouths open, they watched as it found its final resting place—right into a bowl of Caesar salad and its dab of dressing. The middle-aged female patron didn't notice until her next forkful.

A broad smile covered Grandpa's face as she tried to discreetly pull it out with her fingers. She frowned a little, looked around the restaurant, and whispered something to her husband, who merely shrugged and bent over his own plate of food.

"Which Friendly's did you go to?" Trish asked, wondering if anyone might have recognized her children.

But no one was really listening to her. They kept eating and talking and laughing. Only a few biscuits and a little coleslaw remained. Giggles erupted when Mark recounted some story about the geese at the park.

"I got closer than you," Mark stated.

"No, you didn't!" said Jimmy.

Trish interrupted. "Boys, stop arguing. What are you talking about anyway?"

"Grandpa had a rock-throwing contest, and I won," Mark said.

Before Trish could respond, Jimmy voiced his disagreement with his older brother. "No, I did! I threw the rock the best."

Grandpa stayed silent for a few minutes before saying anything. "Boys, you both won," he said matter-of-factly. Instantly, both Mark and Jimmy grinned and stopped picking on one another. Trish wondered what magical powers her dad possessed to stop these all-too-common bouts of male competition.

Just as she started to pick up the dishes and bring them to the sink, Ryan piped up. "Actually, Grandpa won. He hit the big bird first." ❄

"**Shut the door. Do you live in a barn or something?**"

"Grandparents are there to help the child
get into mischief they haven't thought of yet."

GENE PERRET

Sundays with Grandpa

BY AMBER FRANGOS

My plane landed at Cleveland Hopkins International Airport late on a Sunday afternoon. I rented a Dodge Intrepid and drove the sixty-odd miles to my girlhood home to pick up my sons, Roger and Douglas. They had spent the last three weeks visiting Grandma and Grandpa.

With each mile I traveled, my sense of expectation grew. My sons were being exposed to the way of life that I was raised on— church every Sunday, dinner at the dining room table, prayer before every meal, no eating in the living room. These were the kind of values that, with our two-income, fast-paced life, I had not been able to give my sons.

I pulled into the driveway between the tall pines and walked to the side of the house unannounced. I wanted to witness the polish and discipline that my sons now wore. Before I turned the corner in the backyard, I heard the boys giggling and peeked over the side of the upstairs porch.

Both boys were devoid of any clothing and were peeing on the petunias next to the downstairs patio. Grandpa stood at the end of the porch, peacock proud and beaming at the antics of his grandsons. When the boys finished, they took off running in the backyard. Their giggling filled the warm summer breeze.

"Mom!" the boys cried in unison when they saw me.

They ran toward me with all the exuberance that carefree, sun-filled days grant. Two pairs of chubby arms circled my neck.

"Where are your clothes?" I asked.

Both boys shrugged in unconcern and took off running in the backyard. Grandpa waved two pairs of underwear toward them, the boys slipped 'em on, and they took off running again.

"I wish I had half their energy," Grandpa said.

What? No chastising for peeing on Grandma's flowers? No scolding for running outside in your underwear?

"Mom, look what we have!" Roger exclaimed.

Holding what was supposed to be a sand pail, he ran-walked toward me with his brother.

"Grandpa's bullets," Douglas announced. They dropped the pail, and a mound of empty shotgun shells littered the grass.

"We shot Grandpa's gun," both boys said at the same time.

Expecting to get clarification that the boys were in error, I looked at Grandpa.

"You remember the 12-gauge shotgun?" Grandpa asked.

No, I did not remember the 12-gauge or any other gauge gun.

"Stop making that expression or your face will stay like that," Grandpa scolded me. "I supervised."

Like that comment was going to make me feel better!

"You let a four-year-old and a six-year-old shoot a 12-gauge?" I asked.

"We aren't allowed to shoot it without Grandpa holding it for us," Roger explained.

"He makes us close our eyes when he puts it away so we can't find it," Douglas added.

"You know I lock it in the gun safe," Grandpa said.

His look of offense that I would even question him about letting a four-year-old and a six-year-old shoot the 12-gauge bordered on disbelief.

I walked into the television room, and the Cartoon Network blazed in the background.

"Those Ninja Turtles are pretty cute," Grandpa said to me.

At that prompt, my sons took on a karate pose and started wrestling with Grandpa. The trio fell to the floor and knocked the empty pizza box off the coffee table.

"Pizza?" I asked. "On Sunday?"

"It's quicker, and it gives me more time with them," he said.

"You did go to church today, right?" I asked.

"Of course! Why wouldn't we?" Grandpa asked.

"We sang songs and got to stand on the pews," Roger said to me and then explained to his grandpa, "Mom never lets us stand on the pews."

"Grandpa, I gotta go to the bathroom," Douglas said.

"You know the routine," Grandpa stated.

Douglas pulled his underwear off, ran outside to the patio, and watered the flowers once again.

Grandpa's grin filled the room. "That's my boy," he said. "That's my boy." ✺

"No matter where you go, there you are."

*"I have made it a rule never to smoke
more than one cigar at a time."*

MARK·TWAIN

Just like Grandpa Huey

BY LINDA COX

Even though the house has since been remodeled and sold, I can still picture the original white, two-story farmhouse. It sat atop the hill and was just across the field from my parents' home. Surrounded by big trees, Grandpa and Grandma Huey's house always seemed to have a breeze no matter how hot the day. This was the spot where Mom had grown up as a child, so it held special memories for her. Since my daddy farmed the nearby fields, it was only natural that we spent many hours at this house with my grandparents.

Grandpa and Grandma Huey worked hard throughout the Depression years to provide for their two children. Together they managed to keep the farm going even when Grandpa Huey started his own oil company: he delivered fuel oil by horse-drawn wagon.

Grandpa Huey was a tall, slender man with a great sense of humor and a love for people. He had never met a stranger. After those lean years, it was not unusual for a young child to catch Grandpa Huey's eye, and before anyone knew what was happening, my grandfather was reaching into his wallet to give the parents five or ten dollars to buy something for their child.

He never forgot how hard it was during the Depression, and afterward he always wanted to share his blessings with others.

But Grandpa Huey had one very bad habit. Although he was a churchgoing man, he used very colorful language. When that

was coupled with his hot Scotch-Irish temper, his vocabulary was—to use an old expression—enough to make a sailor blush. One thing about it, though, as soon as Grandpa Huey gave vent to his temper, it was over, and he was the teddy bear of a man he normally was. Usually a sheepish, elflike grin would appear on his face, and we'd all know the coast was clear.

Grandpa Huey loved his family more than anything, and, as his precious granddaughter, I was the apple of his eye. His horses were a close second. Even though tractors were used on the farm, he always kept his team of horses and used them for many farm activities. Being stubborn as horses can sometimes be, however, they would occasionally set off Grandpa's temper and bear the brunt of his colorful language. One such incident continues to live on in family lore.

I wish I remembered this incident myself, but I was only four or five years old when it happened. The memories I have of it are from my parents telling the story—over and over and over again. I think it may have been one of their favorite stories about their little girl...

Grandpa Huey and his horses had had one of those days. Apparently his language was loud, very colorful, and full of expletives as he yelled at his horses and used the reins to accentuate what he was trying to get them to do. As always, once Grandpa Huey vented his frustration, he quickly calmed down. When he put the horses away, he gave them special care and some extra hay. However, much to his dismay, that was not the end of this particular incident.

Later, my grandparents and my parents were sitting in the yard, relaxing and enjoying the quiet summer evening under the shade trees. I was playing with my favorite toy, a big wooden rocking horse. It was even fitted with its own leather bridle that Grandpa had fixed for it. I could spend hours rocking on my horse and pretending to be a cowgirl.

Well, I was rocking away and having a grand time when all of a sudden I jumped off my rocking horse and started hitting it with the reins and—you guessed it—repeating all the very colorful expletives Grandpa Huey had used that very afternoon!

(Oh, how I would love to remember the looks on their faces at that very moment!)

Grandma Huey gave Grandpa Huey a talking-to about his conduct in front of little ears while he sat there trying to be duly repentant for what he had done and not laugh. And my mother, once she had shushed my own father's roaring laughter, had a little talk with me about my language and conduct as well.

Something tells me that, when I tired of the rocking horse and ran off to play by myself, the four of them had a very good laugh about the bad habit Grandpa Huey had shared with me that day. Thankfully, the bad habit of Grandpa Huey's language didn't stick with me for very long. And after that memorable afternoon, Grandpa Huey—bless his heart—tried very hard to clean up his language whenever I was around. Well, except where the St. Louis Cardinals were concerned. But that's a story for another day. ❄

"**Your mom and dad won't mind.**"

"I don't know why I did it, I don't know why I enjoyed it, and I don't know why I'll do it again."

SOCRATES

"Pass the Peas, Please"

BY LAURIE RIDDELL

Every summer my mother, my sister, and I crammed our suitcases with everything we needed for the long trek from California to Canada. The train ride lasted forever...three days and two nights. We enjoyed living in the Los Angeles area with tons of friends and neighbors, but we deeply missed our extended family.

My parents had moved away from Toronto to seek a life free of snow, but in the process they left behind parents and siblings—my grandparents, aunts, and uncles. Whenever we undertook the long, arduous trip to see them, we stayed for at least a few weeks at a time. We tried to go as often as possible, but distance and expense made for infrequent visits.

I remember, as I boarded the train, feeling the anticipation of summer adventures with my grandparents in Canada. It must have been hard for my mom to have left such a fun, loving family. But, for those weeks, she became a daughter, and I was enchanted by the joy of family.

I spent those summer visits playing with my sister in the sloping backyard. We stayed away from the forested area in the back because we were told it wasn't safe for little girls, but there was still plenty of fun in the rest of the yard. After hours of outdoor play, we couldn't wait to be called in for dinner.

I washed my hands with soap and rinsed them quickly under cold water. Walking into the dining room, I promptly took my seat at the table covered with a lacy cloth and fancy dishes. Even as a young child, I noticed the muted

floral wallpaper and felt at peace. My grandmother's collection of china cups and saucers stayed safe behind glass doors in her china hutch.

Grandpa sat to my left at the dinner table and appeared to be the perfect dinner guest. He wore suspenders, baggy pants, and a bowtie since he had just come home from work at a department store. He waited patiently for my grandmother to join us.

Once we were all there, he bowed his head to pray and asked God to bless our food.

"Amen," he concluded, lifting his chin.

His mischievous brown eyes shone behind his glasses while we ate our dinner and drank our milk. My sister and I chattered constantly throughout the meal. Thirsty from playing tag all afternoon, I picked up my glass of milk and raised it high to finish the last bit. As I swallowed the creamy liquid, something suddenly bumped into my lips.

I was completely bewildered. What was in my drink?

Sensing something was amiss, my grandmother looked at my grandfather.

"Les...," she warned.

Sitting there innocently enough, he replied with silence and ate another spoonful of peas. He didn't return my grandma's glares.

I banged my glass down and peered into it. My mouth gaped open when I saw what lay at the bottom...a puddle of peas. Then my sister looked in her glass. Same thing! We let out high-pitched squeals of laughter at our discovery! How did those peas get there? It only took a few minutes to realize that my dear grandpa had slipped the intruders into our drinks while we were praying. Even though my grandmother was horrified at the prank, my grandfather just smiled and kept eating his vegetables. ❁

none

"I want to die in my sleep like Grandpa, not like the screaming passengers in his car."

"Elephants and grandchildren never forget."

ANDY ROONEY

Truth or Trout

BY KATHRYN THOMAS

Grandpa Thomas ate my rainbow trout. On purpose. And I held it against him for quite some time.

I adored Dad's parents, but I was grandkid number eleven. Things were different because my oldest cousin was twenty-six years my senior, and there were great-grandkids older than I. That's why any invitation to spend time alone with Grandpa and Grandma was like pink cotton candy at the fair.

One weekend when Dad drove Mom and me to visit Grandpa and Grandma, I thought I had them all to myself. I didn't count on a fish coming between Grandpa and me.

My grandparents spent their retirement years in Truth or Consequences, New Mexico, a big name for a small town on the Rio Grande River. Settled in 1916 as "Hot Springs," the 1950 locals jumped at the chance for fame when Ralph Edwards, host of the popular radio program *Truth or Consequences*, announced he would broadcast the production from the first town that renamed itself after the show. The premise of the program was simple: tell the truth or face the consequences. Today, most folks just call the town "T or C."

My favorite store in T or C was Bullocks, an exciting shopping experience for any kid. On this particular day Grandpa and Dad took me to the sporting-goods section where I chose my first (and only) fishing rod: kid-sized, sleek, and white with a dark-green reel. I was on the fast track to falling in love with the fine art of fishing. Fully stocked, we headed for the river.

The Rio Grande drifts through T or C's desert landscape like a welcome rain shower on a sweltering afternoon. Bordered on the west by the Black Range Mountains, T or C has soil that is basically rock and clay. Tumbleweeds break from their roots to be driven across the ground by autumn's wind. Home to golden eagles, hawks, coyotes, and rattlesnakes, this land remains resistant to man's taming hand, inhospitable to the weak or ill prepared.

Stepping over rocks and across bristly grass, we pushed past scrub and cottonwood trees. I was resolute about staying up with the men. After all, I was the daughter of pioneers.

Settling in a shady spot by the river's edge, I wiggled a slimy worm onto my hook and cast my line just as Grandpa instructed. We settled down to wait.

When my line pulled at my hands and my rod tried to dance away from me, I clutched it with white knuckles while Grandpa and Dad barked orders.

"Hang on! Don't let it get away!"

"Keep the line tight."

"Hold the rod up."

The water broke as a glistening, silver-bellied fish with a reddish, horizontal band shot into the air and thrashed wildly in the midafternoon sun. Irregular black spots on its back and sides added to its beauty. It had freckles just like me!

Weighing at least three or four pounds, it was a whale of a fish for a kid to catch! Grandpa helped me toss the trout into the brush behind us, subdue it, and deposit it in the metal bucket beside us. Filling the pail with water, I kept an eye on my new friend while baiting my hook for the next catch.

As with most beginner's-luck stories, I was the only one who caught a fish that day. Grandpa carried my pole back to the car while I hobbled along with my trout in its watery cage. "Will he be okay until we get him home?"

Grandpa nodded, closing the gap between us on the trail. "Sure will. And he'll be good eating."

I stopped short. "Eating? You can't eat him."

"What do you think we went fishing for? Grandma's going to fry him for dinner."

"No, she's not! He's my pet. I'm taking him home."

Grandpa's laugh wounded me.

I grasped for a logical argument. "He's mine!" was all I could say.

I looked to Dad for support. I didn't get it. "Trout aren't meant to be kept as pets," he said. At least he didn't laugh.

"Grandpa, you can't eat my fish!" I cajoled and protested until I was reduced to sheer begging. Grandpa didn't budge.

Although I told myself he was just teasing me, I cried into the trout's water all the way home.

Somehow Grandpa loosened my grip on the bucket and took it into the house to Grandma. Mom and she praised me for being such a good fisherman. I eagerly looked to them for help in saving my new pet's life. I didn't get it.

I watched in horror as Grandpa sharpened his knife and Grandma got out the skillet. They really were going to kill and eat my fish! I felt like Gretel watching the witch fatten up Hansel. I let the screen door slam behind me as I fled from the kitchen.

Outside, I put my back to the four conspirators as they huddled over my fish. I turned up my nose at the aroma wafting through the mesh wire covering the door. I squeezed my eyes to forestall the tears that welled up at the sound of a knife and fork on a plate.

Looking back now, the truth is—Grandpa was right: we fished in order to eat. The consequence? Because of my naïveté, I suffered much heartache over my trout.

I still have that kid-sized, sleek, white fishing pole. It hangs in the barn with my husband Dan's rods and reels. It's one of my most treasured possessions. Whenever Dan uses my rod, I warn him to be careful with it. After all, Grandpa Thomas bought it just for me—and that makes it and him special. Even if he did eat my rainbow trout. ❄

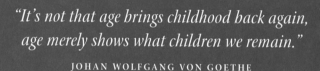

"It's not that age brings childhood back again,
age merely shows what children we remain."

JOHAN WOLFGANG VON GOETHE

The Cat with Two Names

BY MIKE SIMS

Grandpa slowly edged along the back porch of the brick farmhouse. He carried a tray with three glasses of lemonade on it. A young, black-and-white cat—a new addition to the farm—ran back and forth between his feet. Grandpa struggled to not spill the lemonade, but the cat seemed just as determined to trip him. It zipped around the rocking chairs, ran around Grandpa's feet, and then attacked my shoes. Despite all the activity Grandpa managed to give both Grandma and me a tall glass without spilling a drop.

"What's your cat's name, Grandpa?" I asked.

"Cat."

"But what's his name?" I asked again.

"Cat."

The cat, purring loudly, rubbed his head against my jeans.

"Don't you want to give him a real name?"

"He already has two names," Grandpa said matter-of-factly.

Grandma set her drink down on the glass-topped wicker table with a loud clink. We both looked at her. Grandma never made a loud clink.

"What are the two names?"

Grandma looked at Grandpa and interjected, "Why don't you take Mike down to the barn?"

Grandpa looked at his drink. "I want to finish my lemonade."

"What are the two names for the cat? Does he have a first and last name?"

Grandma stood up. "Or you could take him to the gazebo."

Clink. Grandpa put his drink down. "All right."

Grandma stared daggers into Grandpa. "You ought to be able to stay out of trouble down there," she added.

Grandpa stood up and waved at me. We took our drinks down the steps and walked across the vast green lawn. The gazebo stood at the edge of the woods. The smell of pine needles and damp, old wood hung heavy in the air as we climbed up the gazebo steps.

"Now will you tell me the cat's name?" I tripped and spilled all of my lemonade. Grandpa took my glass and set it on the railing next to his.

"Well, the second name is Cat."

"That's a stupid name for a cat, Grandpa."

Grandpa looked around. Grandma was nowhere around.

"That's what your grandma thinks."

"How come she thinks that?"

"We had a deal. She could keep the cat if I could name the cat."

"So she doesn't like the name?"

"Exactly, but the name is what it is, and there's nothing to be done about it."

"What's his first na…" I stopped.

Grandpa had taken his big jackknife out of his pocket and unfolded it.

"Come on. This ought to keep us out of trouble."

He handed me the knife. The blade shone like new because he liked to keep it sharp for barn work. Grandpa shuffled around some old tree branches lying at the edge of the gazebo and pulled a couple of thick old sticks from one.

"I'll teach you how to whittle."

He put a stick in my right hand and held his strong, gnarled hand around mine. With his other hand he squeezed my left hand and the knife. He held the blade— dull side toward us and the sharp side pointing along the stick—so that it was almost lying flat against the piece of wood.

Fizt. Fizt. Fizt. Dragging my small hand along, Grandpa used the strength of his hands to shave most of the bark off in a few quick, powerful strokes .

"Now you try."

When he let go of my hand, I pushed the blade straight down into the stick. Nothing happened. I pushed harder as I held the stick against my stomach.

"Let's try again."

Once again Grandpa held my hands, one on the knife and the other on the stick. He pushed more slowly this time and let me finish each stroke. His hands guided mine to show where each new shave should start. While he seemed to be effortlessly slicing the top off a stick of butter, I struggled just to keep the knife along the edge of the pine.

Once again he let go.

"There. Now you've got it."

I looked up at him and whittled the edge of my thumbnail off.

"Ahh, Grandpa!"

Grandpa just smiled. There wasn't much blood.

"You did fine."

He took my bloody thumb and wiped it on his old jeans. Then he took out a white handkerchief and neatly wrapped it around my thumb. The blood barely showed through.

"There. Now hold this hand in a fist, and I'll show you something to do with your other hand."

Grandpa and I crossed over to the other side of the gazebo. An old dartboard hung on a pine tree a few feet away. The old white posts, the roof, and the flat rail of the gazebo made a perfect frame around the dartboard. Our lemonade glasses sat on the railing off to one corner of the frame.

Grandpa took out his knife again. Then he took out another, smaller knife.

"You need one too."

"For me?"

"Yes. Now watch."

He took his knife by the point, stood straight, aimed, and, with the flick of his wrist, fired his knife right into the target.

Thunk.

Just to the side of the bull's-eye, his big old knife had pierced the dartboard and now was stuck in the tree. He smiled and patted my head.

"You want to learn how to do that."

It was not a question, but I nodded anyway.

Grandpa walked around the gazebo and retrieved his knife. When he got back, I was in firing position.

"Okay, you ready?"

"Yeah, Grandpa."

I flung my new little knife forward and watched it arc up and flop down into the trees.

"Wait. Watch me again," Grandpa said as he took out his own big knife.

Then he looked at me, and just over my shoulder he saw Grandma walking toward us across the grass with a pitcher of fresh lemonade.

Grandpa turned back to the dartboard. He held up his knife, aimed, and started to throw—when suddenly the cat darted across the rail in front of him.

"Grandpa!" Grandma yelled.

Grandpa was too far along. He had launched the knife.

The cat, startled, hissed and sprang off the railing.

Crash!

The lemonade glasses shattered on the ground, and the knife bounced off the side of the target.

"D--- Cat!" Grandpa growled.

Grandpa and I both looked up at Grandma. Standing there in the grass, she gasped and covered her mouth with her free hand. Grandpa just smiled and shook his head.

"That's okay," he said. "That's just his name. Last name, Cat. First name, D---."

Grandma's stare bore into him again as she marched up the steps of the gazebo. Grandpa met her glare with a weak smile.

Grandma took my hand and firmly led me down from the gazebo. She would clean up my thumb properly. As we walked away, Grandpa mumbled that he would clean up the lemonade mess. Looking back across the lawn, I saw him bend down to pick up a piece of sticky glass, and I'm quite sure I heard him say the first and last names of the cat once again.

As I lay in bed the night before we left for home, I received another lecture on being careful, safe, and polite from Grandma as she tucked me in. Afterward, when the lights were out, Grandpa and the cat snuck in together. I sat up, but Grandpa just put a finger to his lips. The cat curled up at my feet; Grandpa gave me a quick hug and left waving a silent "Good night." As I lay back down, I found he'd tucked a little box into bed with me. Inside it was the knife I'd thrown in the woods. The cat purred, and I went to sleep clutching my secret gift. ❄

"*The best baby-sitters, of course, are the baby's grandparents. You feel completely comfortable entrusting your baby to them for long periods, which is why most grandparents flee to Florida.*"

DAVE BARRY

No Smoking!

BY MELISSA FIELDS

Between 1956 and 1976, my good-humored maternal grandparents, Mamaw and Papaw Walker, kept the Camel cigarette company in business with their cigarette consumption. For their six children, however, the rules were perfectly clear: NO SMOKING IN THIS FAMILY—OR ELSE!

They adhered to the "do-as-I-say-not-as-I-do" rule of child-rearing. Of course, my mother, when she was a ten-year-old girl, couldn't resist the temptation to see what smoking was all about, especially when her older cousin, Norman Earle, came for a visit. After all, the few half-smoked cigarettes littering the ground were just asking to be picked up...

"Mom and Dad do this all the time," my mom told Norman reassuringly. "Let's just try it out and see what it's all about. No one will ever know."

They found a couple of previously smoked cigarettes on the ground, snatched them up, and quickly stuffed them into their pockets before anyone could see. Next, they discreetly scoured the house for some matches and pocketed those as well.

Outside the house, they tiptoed around the yard until they reached the chimney on the far side of the old farmhouse. They hid behind it and proceeded to fumble with the matches. It took them several tries to figure out how to light a cigarette.

Just as the spark started burning the end of the cigarette, Papaw rounded the corner. Now, Papaw had a certain tone and depth to his voice that you did not want to hear. If you ever did hear it, you knew it was not a sign of good times ahead. My mom quickly assessed that this was one of those not-so-good occasions. Not a speck of his usual good humor shone in his eyes.

"LOIS ANN WALKER! WHAT...ON...EARTH...IS...GOING... ON...HERE?" he yelled.

My mom and her cousin jumped out of their skins—and Mom nearly swallowed her cigarette in the process.

"Smoking a cigarette?! What have I told you about smoking a cigarette?" Papaw ranted. "It is not allowed, and I will not have my children doing it in my home or on my property. Get rid of it now, and don't you ever let me catch you smoking again!"

Well, that was all Lois and Norman needed to hear.

"Yes, sir," they replied respectfully.

To this day, neither she nor her cousin has ever touched another cigarette.

Fast-forward twenty years...

Even with grandchildren running around the farmhouse, Mamaw and Papaw still kept the profits rolling for the Camel cigarette company. All of us grandkids were amazed because we all knew "THE RULE." Although we saw cigarettes dangling from their mouths, we were not allowed to go near one of those white sticks.

One bright fall day while Mamaw was in the kitchen cooking and Papaw was out mowing with the tractor, my brother Doug and cousin Bryan decided to risk the wrath of Papaw. The two curious ten-year-olds snuck into Mamaw's purse and grabbed two brand-new cigarettes. Then, thinking no one would ever know what they were up to, they tiptoed out to the smokehouse.

In all the excitement of lighting up, they never heard the tractor pull up and stop. The front door of the smokehouse opened, and in walked Papaw. He took one look at Bryan. He took one look at Doug. He opened his mouth to speak just as Doug and

Bryan began to choke on their first drag. They knew what was coming. And Papaw knew that they knew what was coming.

"Boys!" Papaw started.

Oh no! Here it comes, Doug and Bryan thought at the same moment.

"Boys!" he said again, as they both continued choking on the smoke.

He saw the total fear in their eyes. However, in all their fright, they failed to notice that Papaw's eyes were glimmering with his usual good humor.

"Boys," he began again, not missing a beat.

He continued to walk right through the building to the backdoor.

"Just don't burn down my smokehouse."

With that, he walked right out the back of the smokehouse, and to this day, Doug and Bryan—just like my mom and her cousin before them—have never touched another cigarette. ✳

"Here's a quarter. Don't spend it all in one place."

> *"I'm saving that rocker for the day*
> *when I feel as old as I really am."*
>
> DWIGHT D. EISENHOWER

Doggone Trouble!

BY PAULA J. MILLER

Doggone it! Those pesky varmints have been at it again!" Grandpa exclaimed in exasperation.

He pushed his gray Stetson back on his forehead and stood disgustedly in his backyard. Then he reached into the front pocket of his snap-button western shirt and pulled out a pouch of tobacco.

"Who's been at what again?" My sisters and I asked, coming to stand beside him.

"Those dogs," he muttered, pulling his pipe out and filling it with a wonderful cherry-scented tobacco.

He pointed to the garbage cans lying on the ground. "That's the third time this week."

Grandpa's backyard was fenced in with a beautiful, redwood fence. His backyard bordered an alleyway, and his garbage cans lay in disarray, their contents strewn across the alley and onto the street.

"And you can bet each one of them took a pee on the cans too!" he growled. Then he turned and winked at us. "Let's go get a piece of candy and think on this for a bit."

He peeked around the corner to make sure Grandma was busy watering her flowers and then led us to the secret stash in the cupboard above the fridge. He pulled out a handful of Root Beer Barrels and Butterscotch Buttons and gave them to us. Their sweetness dissolved on our tongues. We all sat for a bit, thinking.

"I know!" he said suddenly.

He went to the carport and pulled out some bungee cords. In a matter of minutes, he had the garbage cans upright and strapped to the fence. He stood back to admire his work and, tugging on his suspenders, said more to himself than to us, "That oughta keep them out of trouble."

But the next morning the cans were in the same mess they were before.

"Some folks just don't know how to keep their animals on a leash," Grandpa grumbled.

He led us back to the candy cupboard while we scratched our heads.

Then I saw it. His clear-blue German eyes started to sparkle. He chuckled out loud, then a bit louder. The shrewd farmer sprang into action.

"This will get 'em for sure," he stated with a touch of menace.

Grandpa worked all afternoon setting up his trap. A little wire here, a little wire there, and he was done. He sat back on his haunches and slapped a leg. "Boy, this will be something to see!"

That night, after the sun settled behind the Idaho mountains, he sat and waited with one ear cocked toward the door. Sure enough, the little pack of garbage-can-peeing-canines came strutting down the alley and headed straight for Grandpa's neat row of cans. A few nonchalant sniffs and some lifted legs revealed that the dogs were unaware of what awaited. But the electric fence they peed on sent them yipping across town.

"Hee-hee!" Grandpa laughed as he watched the dogs tear down the street as if their backsides were on fire.

"I've never seen a dog run so fast in my life!" I hollered with approval.

Grandpa pushed his gray Stetson a bit farther back on his head and pulled his pipe out of his smiling mouth.

"I bet you could hear 'em all the way across town!" Grandpa bragged.

He tapped a bit of cherry tobacco in the end of the pipe and lit it expertly. Then he looked at us and winked, his eyes sparkling with pure, unadulterated mischief. He had won! ❄

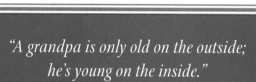

"A grandpa is only old on the outside; he's young on the inside."

ANONYMOUS

Practically a Joker

LAUREL SEILER BRUNVOLL

I jumped out of the car and almost ran up the front walkway to my parents' home. I rang the doorbell, expecting my grandfather to answer, but instead the door creaked open very slowly. Cautiously, I stepped into the foyer. *How strange. No one is here to greet us.*

"Hello?" I called as my husband caught up to me.

Just as he started to say something, I saw movement out of the corner of my eye. My grandfather barreled out of his hiding place and grabbed me into a big bear hug while I let out a scream.

His warm laughter enveloped me and slowed down my racing heart. "Even though you scared me to death, it's good to see you, Grandpa," I announced.

My husband gave him a hearty handshake and laughed with him. "You got us good." He glanced over to the string tied to the doorknob and shook his head without saying anything more.

It was hard to believe that more than three months had already elapsed since my grandmother's death. My grandfather's adaptability in life was never more evident to me as when he moved in with my parents. He still laughed and smiled, and he seemed genuinely content in my parents' home.

What I loved most about Grandpa was his positive outlook on life and his true joy in living, even in his darkest days. He faithfully lived out one of his favorite sayings: "You cannot choose what happens to you in life, but you can choose how you are going to react."

Later, while seated around the dinner table, we enjoyed a feast of roast beef, mashed potatoes, and lots of gravy. Joke-telling abounded. Grandpa loved to end his exclamatory remarks with "Sock, deer!" Then my dad chimed in with his Green Bay-isms. I couldn't even finish swallowing my food, I was laughing so hard.

I got up to help my mom and my sister, Becky, clear away the dishes. My grandfather didn't budge. He waited for my mom to come near. "Where's the payoff?" he asked, banging the table with knife and fork in hand.

"It's coming," she replied with a smile. She knew he could smell the homemade cherry pie cooling off in the kitchen. Becky grabbed a few plates and presented his "payoff" with a little mock curtsy.

Just as he was licking the red-stained plate of its remains, Becky took a quick breath and spoke up. "Grandpa, it's really important for you to stay off ladders." She recounted how she had caught him trying to change a lightbulb earlier in the day. My parents quickly agreed with her. No one wanted to see him fall. No one wanted to see an eighty-seven-year-old with Parkinson's disease get hurt. No one thought he should climb any ladder rungs for that matter.

Grandpa promised to be careful. He promised to be good. He promised to do what they requested. But I thought I saw a tiny gleam in his blue eyes.

The following day, while our parents were at work, Becky went upstairs to study in her bedroom. She had to learn some new kinesiology terms for her physical-therapy class. Shortly after she got settled, though, she was startled by a faint voice from off in the distance.

"Help..."

She looked up, sat still, and listened carefully.

"Help..."

She heard it again, only a little louder. As she recognized the voice, her heart started to beat faster.

"Can someone help me?"

She threw her thick book to the floor and jumped up off the bed. She flew down the stairs and ran toward the sound of that familiar voice in trouble. She skipped the last few steps and landed with a loud thud. Her heart racing, she glanced quickly in the living room, dining room, and kitchen before she found his body lying on the floor of his room.

"Grandpa!"

His motionless back was to her, and, thinking the worst, she burst out into tears. Five more steps. Still no movement. Just as her hand reached down to him, he turned over and looked up.

"Help me! He's biting my toe," Grandpa said without any hint of a smile. My sister stared in disbelief at the rubber alligator biting his toe.

Her watery eyes remained focused on the alligator for a few more seconds. Then her whole body started shaking as she cried harder. He slowly got up and tentatively reached out to hug her. His strong arms circled her with an unspoken apology. Even though she felt relieved, the truth still hadn't fully sunk in— Grandpa was just pulling another one of his pranks! ❄

"All I got for Christmas was an orange."

"It's never too late to have a happy childhood."

JERRY SEINFELD

Pawzie

CHRISTINE CONNELL THRON

Ash the Bash with all the Cash!" As my father's booming voice called to my daughter, Ashley broke into a broad grin. She was used to this greeting from Pawzie, the grandfather name he had chosen for himself.

My father was a loud, cheerful Irishman. He was the fifth of six children—five of whom were boys, and all of them were loud. When we'd meet for family reunions, the noise was deafening at times, but it was a nice loud. Hearty laughter would bounce off the walls, interrupted only when one of the brothers yelled something to get the next guffaw started.

Pawzie's cheerful disposition was a gift to our family. He was always upbeat even though circumstances were not always wonderful. After all, life is life. But one of his favorite sayings was "Life is just a bowl of cherries." Eventually, when I had a family of my own, I told him that I was annoyed with him for the saying—it had left me totally unprepared for life. He simply smiled...

One day I was so surprised to hear my young son, Andrew, say to me, "I don't like Pawzie."

I was shocked. Everyone liked Pawzie. He was the most lovable guy on the planet. "Why on earth don't you like Pawzie?" I asked with a touch of incredulity.

"He always calls me 'Podna,'" he replied, "and my name is Andrew. What's a 'podna' anyway?"

I snickered. Andrew was right. It wasn't long after "Ash the Bash with all the Cash" that Pawzie came up with "Hiya, podna!"

"That's his way of greeting you," I explained. "It means 'Hey, partner.' You know, like a pal."

"I still don't like it," he said.

When I explained the problem to my father, he chuckled, apologized to Andrew, and called him by his name until Andrew warmed up to "Podna" sometime later. This took awhile because we, like so many other families today, lived many miles from the grandparents. For us, it was eleven hundred miles. Even so, I was determined to have my parents be part of my children's lives, so we traveled to their home twice a year, and they came to ours once a year for as long as they were able. Over the years, my father worked his funny and sweet ways right into my children's hearts.

So when he'd call, "Hey, come on over here and sit on Pawzie's lap," there was no hesitation. And just before they'd climb up, he'd delight in dislodging his dentures and smiling at them. They'd smile back, climb up, and request a repeat performance, which he obligingly granted.

If there was fun to be had, Pawzie was in. During one of his visits to our house, we got a hefty amount of snow. Being from New Orleans, he had never been sledding.

"Have a turn, Pawzie," I suggested.

It was funny to see a skinny, gray-haired man in his seventies taking a turn on the sled for the first time in his life, much to the pleasure of his adoring audience.

One of my very favorite pictures of him, however, is from one of our visits to New Orleans.

I walked into the yard where he was with my two oldest children.

"Hiya, darlin'," he called to me.

"What are all of you doing?" I asked through my laughter.

All three of them had the biggest grins on their faces, and I had the camera. Pawzie is sitting in a lawn chair holding "Ash the Bash with all the Cash" at age three. My son, Jonathan, at age five, is standing to his right. Ashley is wearing Pawzie's eyeglass case on her hand like a mitten, and all three have cigars sticking out of their mouths. It's the best picture—because that was the Pawzie we all loved and adored.

It was a great loss to our family when Pawzie passed away. He was a person with contagious joy who lived life richly and in line with his priorities. His joy lives on in me each time I walk by that picture—and can't help but smile. ✼

"Do it right the first time."

*"Every generation revolts against its fathers
and makes friends with its grandfathers."*

LEWIS MUMFORD

Trick or Treat?

DONNA NORDQUIST

Knock...Knock...Knock...

My two sons raced each other to the door. It was Halloween night, and Grandma and Grandpa always came for the traditional trick-or-treating event. They stayed at the house to hand out candy so that we as a family could go out trick-or-treating with neighborhood friends.

Tyler and Ryan whipped open the door. Grandma and Grandpa quickly filled the room with excitement, hugs, and kisses. I, on the other hand, was frantic. I attempted to gather the missing costume pieces and find batteries for the nonworking flashlights. (They never seemed to work on Halloween night!)

"All right, boys, let's sit down and eat some pizza," Grandma coaxed. "You need something in your stomachs before you go out trick-or-treating."

Everyone, except me, sat around the table. The aroma of pizza and the sound of goofy laughter filled the air. I grabbed a piece to eat on the run as I continued collecting things for our night.

Ding...Dong...

Grandma left the table to answer the door. While she handed out candy to several trick-or-treaters, the rest of the gang kept eating more pizza. Grandpa leaned in close to Tyler and Ryan and whispered, "You know, when I was a young boy-child, I had quite a night one Halloween."

My sons' eyes widened, and they nestled closer to him. His soft voice and sly smile promised a very good story. They sat still and listened.

"Well, one Halloween night a long time ago, I went trick-or-treating with my friends. We went to Jimmy Jones's house and rang the bell. Jimmy Jones opened his door, threw a bucket of ice-cold water on us, and yelled, 'Trick or Treat! Ha...Ha...Ha...Ha!'

"We just stood there, drenched, with ice-cold water dripping from our costumes. That was when we decided to get Jimmy Jones back. We got a brown lunch bag and carefully placed some nice, fresh dog poop in the paper bag. Then we went back to Jimmy Jones's house and placed it on the front steps. We lit the bag on fire, rang the bell, and ran for cover. Jimmy Jones opened the door and saw a paper bag on fire."

Grandpa paused and sat back with the satisfied grin of a mischievous young boy.

"Then Jimmy Jones stomped on the bag over and over again to get the fire out and...surprise...he got covered with POOP!!"

At that last word, I heard my mother yell, "Donnnnnnnnnn!"

"What do you think you're doing?" she said as she, completely shocked, entered the dining room.

I walked into the kitchen and saw Tyler and Ryan laughing so hard they couldn't even catch their breath. My husband sat in disbelief; he was at a total loss for words.

"What are they laughing about?" I asked him.

"You don't want to know," he replied.

Grandma took a long look at Grandpa as he continued to chuckle. Her unhappiness with Grandpa's story combined with his mirth only made the peanut gallery at the table laugh harder.

"You need to go in the family room for a time-out for the rest of the night and think about what kind of stories you're telling a five- and an eight-year-old," Grandma directed.

I finally managed to find the batteries for the flashlights and gather the trick-or-treat bags. The boys were still laughing as four of us bolted toward the front door. Grandma gave us her warm good-byes.

"Boys, do you need a brown bag?" Grandpa called out from the family room.

"Don!" is all we heard as we walked out the door. Tyler and Ryan ran across the front lawn to their group of buddies and immediately started bragging about their grandpa's Halloween trick. As I approached the children huddled together, I tried to stop their story, but it was too late! More than one kid wanted to "try that joke on someone."

After hours of fun gathering candy, we returned home with heavy bags bulging with chocolates, candies, and sours. We rang one last doorbell—our own home. Grandma peeked out the side window and let us into the warm, toasty house.

"Where's Grandpa?" Tyler and Ryan asked Grandma.

"Grandpa's been in time-out while you've been out trick-or-treating," Grandma said.

"Wow, Grandpa was in a time-out for all that time!" exclaimed Ryan.

"I've never been in a time-out for that long," said Tyler incredulously.

Grandma smiled, hugged the boys, and invited them to go to their grandfather. They entered the family room and found Grandpa sitting in a big green leather chair, comfortably rocking away. He was happy to see them and gave them a big squeeze. As I looked over at my dad, I knew, without a doubt, that he had had plenty of time to remember more young boy-child stories to tell his grandchildren. When I glanced at my mom's smiling face, I knew she was enjoying every minute of this night. ❄

"I walked ten miles in the snow to school every day, up hill, both ways."

"*If you cannot get rid of the family skeleton, you may as well make it dance.*"

GEORGE BERNARD SHAW

Don't Scratch My Back

BY TERI HORSLEY

N ow listen here, Suzie," my grandpa said forcefully to one of his first customers. "This back massager is just what you need to make you young again."

I had just entered the garage, the site of my grandpa's annual junk sale, when I heard him giving this poor woman one of his best sales pitches ever. He had this dilapidated massage tool in one hand and a gray-haired customer in the other.

Suzie, as he called her, was trying to pull away, but he would not let go. "You gotta take this home with you, honey. You need it," he said.

From prior experience, I knew that Suzie should just give up and hand him her money. I had seen Grandpa in action before. When he said someone had to have something, he did not stop until the person accepted that fate and purchased the object. The process took longer with some people, but it always ended the same way.

"Now listen, Suzie," Grandpa continued. "I am the man I am today because I used to use this fine piece of equipment regularly." He stood tall with his chest puffed out.

"In fact," he said, without giving her a chance to respond, "I have stayed so young that my hair hasn't even begun to turn gray, and I'm almost seventy."

I hid my dismay and quickly glanced around the garage to see if anyone else had taken notice of this inflammatory declaration. What Grandpa didn't mention to her was that his hair was not gray because he regularly took an eyebrow pencil and dyed all three of the hairs remaining on his head.

"But, sir, I don't need a massager," pleaded the woman.

I didn't know whether to laugh or cry as I saw this cornered customer struggling with my very large grandpa.

"Now, honey, you can call me Ben," he said. "Let's give 'er a try. Don't this feel great?"

My mouth dropped open as he began to rub this thing up and down the woman's back. The next thing I knew, the woman was squealing like a little girl. Grandpa continued his massage.

"I'm only willing to sell you this fine back rubber because I think it can help you," laughed Grandpa. "I promise you, this thing will put a spring back in your step."

Her face reddened as her body twisted and turned. I honestly think I saw the return of that spring in her step. Grandpa was delighted to see immediate results, but then he must have seen the horror on my face. He finally stopped assaulting the woman with his back massager. I was silently praying she didn't call the police when she suddenly reached into her purse and pulled out her wallet.

"You know, Ben, I think I do feel better," she said. "Do you think it would work if I use it with heat?"

"Well, sure, honey," he said with a smile. "That is just what you need."

She then handed him five dollars and headed out the door.

I was finally able to breathe again after the woman left. As Grandpa began to tell me what a fine salesman he was, the color was returning to my cheeks. I thought the whole episode was finally over when Grandpa suddenly stopped and looked me square in the eye:

"You know, Toot, I sure do hope that thing works when she takes it home and plugs it in!" ❄

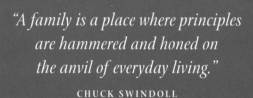

"*A family is a place where principles are hammered and honed on the anvil of everyday living.*"

CHUCK SWINDOLL

Free Spirit

TERESA HAUGH

W e're going to town after a while to get a slaw dawg,"
my grandfather Gordon announced.

It was Friday night, and on Friday nights my
grandfather always took my grandmother Eva to get a hotdog
with coleslaw on it. It was tradition.

I was sitting in my grandparents' living room, happy to be
visiting with them. My "papaw" was strong and wiry with a head
of beautiful white hair. He was dressed in dark pants and a cotton
shirt that buttoned up the front. My sweet grandmother, who
stood a little taller than he did, was wearing a cotton dress and a
matching fabric belt. Her outfit was fashionable for the 1960s, at
least as fashionable as it needed to be for eating slaw dogs.

"May we go with you?" I asked, hopefully.

"We" included my cousin Vicki. I knew if the two of us were
lucky enough to go to town with them, we could probably spend
the night too. For me, nothing was more fun than staying
overnight at my grandparents' house.

Each morning Grandma would walk out onto the back porch in
her nightgown to fetch a bottle of milk. She refused to listen to that

"confounded refrigerator" hum all night, so she made Papaw move it outside on the porch next to the washing machine and the firewood. Most evenings Papaw sat in front of the potbellied stove reading a Zane Grey novel with his fat puppy lying in his lap, but on Wednesdays he and Grandma went to church, and on Fridays they drove into town.

"You have to ask your mother if you can go," Papaw told me.

Before he had a chance to reconsider, I ran outside to find my parents. I was sure they would let me stay over. Visits to the hills of North Carolina to see our extended family didn't happen often, and they knew that a trip to town with Papaw would be a highlight of my summer vacation.

I cautiously made my way down the high steps of Papaw's house. Seeing daylight between the stair steps always made me nervous. The ground seemed to be twenty feet below my little legs. When I was even younger, I had to crawl backwards on my hands and knees to get down off the porch.

When I reached the ground safely, I glanced up the hill and saw my dad and Uncle Jim. I headed their way to convince them of my plans to spend the night. As I got closer, I saw them inspecting Papaw's old '49 Chevy. Papaw always left the car backed off the gravel road at the top of the hill, resting up against a bank of rich, black dirt. He wanted the car to be pointed in the right direction when it was time to take off again.

"Look at this green paint right here," said my dad, pointing to the front bumper.

"What is it?" asked Uncle Jim.

My dad laughed deeply from his belly. "That's from the time Gordon stopped the car when his brakes didn't work."

"What!?"

"Yep, he drove all the way down the mountain and into town, but he didn't have any brakes. When he got there, the only way he could stop was to run into the Sinclair dinosaur sign at the gas station," my dad explained.

Jim laughed and shook his head in disbelief, but the dinosaur's green paint mark left no doubt that the story was true.

"Do you think he'll ever hurt himself or Eva driving that car?"

"Well, he always makes it back in one piece," said my dad. "And Eva doesn't know any better."

My grandmother who had never driven herself, really didn't know that her husband's driving feats were legendary. And my dad and Jim weren't about to tell their father-in-law how to drive.

Gordon was a free spirit. He wasn't likely to take too well to anyone telling him what to do, even family.

"Well, we can't tell them about this," said my dad. "They'll just worry."

I knew "them" was my mother and aunt. They wouldn't want to know Papaw was flying down the mountain roads without brakes on the car. Uncle Jim agreed. With a final smile and a shake of their heads, my dad and uncle went about their business.

I snuck away quietly. Maybe it was not the best time to tell my dad I wanted to ride in that car. I found "them," my mom and my aunt, and got their permission for Vicki and me to stay overnight.

Later in the afternoon, after some hugs and kisses, Vicki and I finally sent our parents on their way. We ran back into the house where Grandma was gathering up her purse and putting on her shoes. Papaw was looking for the car keys. I braved the rickety front steps once again, and Vicki and I ran up the hill to the car. We pulled open the door and climbed gingerly into the backseat.

I looked askance at Vicki. I noticed the floorboard in the backseat had holes in it. She wasn't concerned. She lived near our grandparents, and she was experienced in riding in the Chevy. She crawled over me into the back of the car, rested her back against the cracked leather seat, and stretched her short legs forward until her feet were propped against the back of the seat in front of her.

"Just don't let your legs dangle," she said matter-of-factly.

I jumped in beside her and slouched down until my feet reached the front seat.

Grandma got in the car as if she were a royal lady going to the opera. Papaw slid behind the wheel, turned the key, and cranked the engine. He rolled his window down, and we were off.

Looking through the holes in the floorboard and watching the road fly by under my feet was great fun. It was like a roller-coaster ride as Papaw took us merrily down the twisting mountain road. As he steered the old car around the curves, we leaned first to the left and then to the right. He hung his head out the window and watched the gravel fly by as the tires crunched along the road. Claiming he couldn't see out of it, Papaw never used the windshield. And it made perfect sense to Grandma for Grandpa to drive with his head hanging out the window.

"You can have a Coke with ice" was all Papaw said to us on the way to town. That was good enough for me. I was just glad to be along for the ride.

Papaw Gordon was the first truly liberated person I ever met. He was himself, and he lived life his own way. His spirit made him great, and I pray that God allowed a little of Grandpa's free spirit to be passed on to me. ❄

*"You know you're getting old when
the candles cost more than the cake."*

BOB HOPE

Fields of Honey Wheat

BY KEVIN WORKMAN

Each summer, work and weather seemed to chisel him away. At my young age, I knew little of hard work, but my grandpa was sure to impress upon me its values. Lines and scars wrote stories on his hands, telling of the endless number of fields they toiled. One day I would look across waving fields of golden wheat and deeply appreciate all the men who worked the ground and carried its brown mark underneath their fingernails, just as my grandpa did.

I grew up just outside the shadows of Kansas City skyscrapers. In the summertime, our family would often pile into our Ford van and drift like floating cotton across a sea of farmland to Nebraska. I'd look out my window and watch the highway gradually change from faded black in Missouri to a tinted red in Nebraska. This meant we were getting close to Grandpa's farm. Finally, a half-mile driveway snaked its way up to the familiar yellow house. I was always excited to close this last stretch of distance between adventure and me.

My earliest memories recall spending lazy afternoons capturing frogs and turtles, taunting the livestock, or making forts and mud pies wrapped in lamb's ear leaves. However, those days of carefree wonder seemed to pass all too quickly. Before I knew it, my summer vacations became summer jobs. I was taught to drive the tractor, which scared me to a paler skin tone. And the livestock and I didn't seem to understand each other very well. Grandpa would stand in the feedlot and yell, "Su-su-su-su-cow!" I'm not sure what that meant in bovine tongue, but as if on cue, the cows would eagerly trot toward him with an obvious look of anticipation. The cows never actually ran unless they saw me. A full-speed chase would then occur. That aggression has, to this day, kept me looking over my shoulder in a pasture.

Even though I often felt as if I was not fit for farm work, Grandpa believed every boy should learn certain skills with his hands. For instance, putting up fence posts. By the time I was nine, he had me drive so many stakes I probably set the record for the fastest stake driving around. (Of course, Grandpa himself was probably hauling a stake driver around when he was still in swaddling clothes.) But I admit, driving pole after pole into the hard earth left me with a sense of accomplishment. I even enjoyed the hard work somewhat.

Despite any pleasure I derived from fence building, I hated electric fences. Although it isn't alive, an electric fence could sneak up and attack without warning, leaving a jolting impression, instilling fear from head to toe.

When it came to the recreational hours of the day, Grandpa was an easygoing fellow. He never passed up a bowl of ice cream or a game of cards after dinner. He loved having Grandma as his partner in cards...or rather crime. The two of them spoke in code with mere eye contact. Still, we tried to win—and occasionally they let us.

But despite his easygoingness, Grandpa always put work first. If I ever decided to slack off a bit, punishment was harsh and swift. I'd sometimes sneak a break anyway. There were just too many things for a thirteen-year-old to notice on a summer day, and I couldn't just let those opportunities slip by. In fact, I soaked them in. Often I would steal away to the pond and, lying in the grass, watch dragonflies trace the outlines of clouds. Throughout my teenage years I migrated back to the farm like clockwork. A few more summers passed, and little hairs started sprouting from my chin. Grandpa began paying wages for my labor—and the labor intensified. For example, I was soon introduced to thistle cutting. Grandpa would swing his hoe with an experienced arc and remove root from soil in one fell swoop. I, on the other hand, chopped away until blisters formed a colony on my palm. In time I became more efficient with my energy. I also invested in my own pair of leather gloves. Just as soon as I mastered thistle cutting, Grandpa recruited me to "walk beans," a chore that involved using a sharp hook to cut nuisance plants from the bean field.

Summers had definitely changed. I now woke before the sun and, several back-breaking hours later, watched it slip down behind my bent-over body out in some field. Grandpa would now be a speck on the horizon of the bean field, leaving me to work more and more on my own. Our hoes and corn knives thrashed in unison as, shining in the sun, they sought out and dispatched intruding weeds. I remember the sweat dripping down my spine. These days seemed endless. I peered into my water jug at the floating particles of dirt and grass and quite gratefully poured its lukewarm contents down my throat. I couldn't imagine a whole lifetime like this, but as I looked across the field at my stubborn grandpa hacking at stubborn weeds, I didn't need to imagine it. I just watched him.

Every evening we'd arrive home to a cadence of our heavy rubber boots being dragged across the porch while crickets played their evening music. On the table a home-cooked meal, featuring a bounty from the garden, awaited. Grandma presented steaming dishes of meats and vegetables. Grandpa liked corn picked fresh from the field and his milk thick and not skimmed. And he  always used fresh honey instead of sugar on his food. He clearly enjoyed the fruits of his labor.

Not only did Grandpa enjoy his bounty, he was a strong believer in not wasting anything. This meant my plate had to be practically licked clean—but that implicit assignment was no problem after a long day's work. However, there were exceptions to my way of polishing off dinner, and those happened when Grandma was absent and Grandpa was forced to do the cooking. The result was always a very ugly display of culinary expression. He called it pea soup. It was simply mashed peas, water, salt, and pepper. The sight and smell of the concoction made me gag, but Grandpa insisted I devour his soup. I attempted a single bite and failed to swallow the thick, hot, green mush. Needless to say, I went without lunch that day.

I think Grandpa's belief in not wasting anything was actually an obsession. Evidence? The row of pine trees that blocked the north wind from the house hid a collection of Grandpa's artifacts. Things he couldn't bring himself to discard, such as three old cars, four pop machines, six pieces of out-of-date farm equipment, and many other rusty odds and ends. The only purposes these things ever served were to aid my young adventures and to house field mice. I was told in my later years that Grandpa would even eat my unwanted baby food so it wouldn't go to waste. It was probably peas.

The last summer of hard work finally came and quickly began to fade. Fall began breathing cool kisses down my neck. I began to feel a sense of genuine accomplishment. The crops were turning golden, and so were the leaves. Soon the combines would be out harvesting underneath that huge full moon and its half smile. Giant buffaloes, spread across the ancient prairies, were peacefully grazing.

The trees slowly undressed to expose their graceful tangles. The fields yielded their produce. Only a few lonely corn stalks stood shaking in the wind. The crows spied from above for leftover grain. The traces of our summer work were scavenged. Snow painted a new world.

I returned home for the start of a new school year. On my head, a seed company hat stained with sweat. On my lips, a faint taste of salt. In my stride, a newly gained knowledge and strength. Sometimes I would doze in class and wake under a bright blue sky stretching over endless fields of honey wheat; the summer sun conducting an orchestra of cicadas and soaring barn swallows.

I knew I would probably never be a farmer, but my grandpa had shown me something beautiful in something simple. I knew I would always return to the rolling hills of farmland to smell the air and reconnect with my memories of working by his side.

Besides, those summers at the farm helped me learn some things that aren't learned inside the classroom or in the house. I've learned that some men spend their lives on the same old acres because something within keeps calling them there. Through old, insightful eyes they see something the average city boy doesn't. When it rained, Grandpa would simply say, "God has answered our prayers." I wish all I wanted was rain. ❄

"Don't count your chickens before they hatch."

"You're more trouble than the grandchildren!" is the greatest compliment a grandparent can receive.

GENE PERRET

This Little Piggy

BY MARY KAY MOODY

We crunched up the gravel drive to Joe's parents' farm. Joe parked the car and no sooner than he slid the front seat forward, Davey jumped out into the thin January sun. Like a typical three-year-old boy, he headed straight for a dirty clump of leftover snow at the edge of the drive. Stomp, stomp! Splat, splat! Grin.

"I'm going to see the *piggies*," he hollered as he ran toward the barn. I looked at Joe and he looked at me with raised eyebrows. We took a synchronized deep breath. He'd be back.

Joe held the sagging gate open for me, and we crossed the cobbled path through Gram's garden, studded with the stubble and skeletons of late zinnia plants she hadn't cleaned out before winter hit. We wiped our feet on the back-porch rug and entered a new world. While the January afternoon outside offered pale sunlight, a damp chill, and images in black and white, the kitchen was cheery with warmth, laughter, and delicious aromas.

Grampa Kurt leaned his elbow on the old Formica table. "Howdy, kids. Where's Davey?"

Grampa Kurt was a big man and all farmer with his ruddy cheeks, layers of flannel, and clunky boots. And he loved a good laugh, especially whoopee-cushion-type jokes. His eyes sparkled, and his thin lips tried to hold back grins during his constant, good-natured teasing.

Joe gave a half smile. "The barn. Went to see the pigs."

Gram at her wood-burning cookstove peered over her shoulder. "Uh-oh."

We all nodded. Just then the screen door slammed. The kitchen door opened, and Davey ran in, eyes like saucers.

"Grampa Kurt, where are the piggies? They're not in the barn!" he asked anxiously.

A collective inhalation left the room startlingly quiet. We looked to Grampa.

"Well, son. It's like this." He looked to Gram.

Nobody was bailing him out of this one.

Grampa wrapped his hands around his coffee. "Son, we killed 'em. That's..."

Davey's hands flew to his hips. He stomped a booted foot. "You can't kill the piggies! If you kill pigs, I'm never coming to see you again!"

I studied my son.

Tears ran down his face as he dashed through the silent kitchen. I followed. He threw himself, face first, onto Gram's old brown tweed couch and sobbed.

I rubbed his back, sat him up, slipped off his coat, and then let him cry himself out. A while later he turned over, cheeks flaming as they always did when he cried. "Why'd he have to kill 'em, Mom?" he said with a sniffle.

"Honey, that's why Grampa raises them."

"But I love them."

"I know."

His lower lip went out. "I wanted to play with 'em."

I nodded. "I know. But they had grown a lot since you were here last. They were too big to play with." I stood him up. "About this big," I said as I touched his shoulder.

His eyes grew large. "Really?"

"Yeah. They grow faster than you do." I brushed his straw-colored hair off his forehead. "Kind of big to play with."

"Oh." He plopped on the couch and worked his lips. Thinking. I waited.

A minute later he sighed and looked at me. "Think I'll go play with the cat." He started to walk away—and then spun around. "He won't kill the cat, will he?"

I chuckled. "No, honey, he won't kill the cat."

"Good."

Davey slipped his coat on as he walked through the kitchen. "I'm goin' out to play with the cat."

A half hour later the teasing aromas of Gram's kitchen had culminated into a tasty dinner, and I called Davey in from the barn.

He walked in, smiling, and was half out of his coat before he closed the door. "What's for dinner?"

I pinned Grampa Kurt with a glare.

He bit his lips before he said, "Pork tenderloin and Gramma's mashed potatoes. Wash your hands."

Rare he'd pass up an opportunity to tease. I smiled my thanks. ❋

"There's no crying in baseball."

"The best place to be when you're sad is Grandpa's lap."

AUTHOR UNKNOWN

"Hen-REE!"

SHELLEY HOUSTON

Grandma watched Grandpa every minute. Mom said that Grandpa used to drink and carouse. I didn't really know what either of those words meant, but I was pretty sure that if Grandpa had done it, I would have liked it.

My parents separated when I was four, so Mom and we three kids moved in with my grandparents, Henry and Elizabeth McClain. Our lives became secure in their little two-bedroom house.

Dinner there often consisted of cornbread and beans, accompanied by bounty from the garden. Next, Mom scooted us into the tub for a hot bath, followed by clean jammies. Then came my favorite part: I'd claim my spot on Grandpa's lap and lay my head on his chest as he sat in his rocker. Just Grandpa and me. We didn't need to talk; the silence was comfortable. He rocked me and rubbed my back as the smell of fresh tobacco in his pocket tickled my nose.

Grandpa said he needed me for various chores around the house, and I was always ready to help. I pulled weeds—and maybe a few flowers too—and I helped burn the trash and prune the trees. Grandpa's peach tree, sitting smack-dab in the middle of the front lawn, displayed plump, juicy peaches that were the envy of the neighborhood. One day, though, Grandpa took me to the side yard and showed me his nectarine tree. He explained that it had superior quality because it was a high-bred peach and that it was his prized possession. I shared that pride and preference from then on.

Well, Grandpa loved to play jokes as much as he loved nectarines. Once, we all went for a visit to Uncle Andy's farm in Oklahoma. On our first morning there, Grandpa and Uncle got up before dawn to feed the animals. I just knew they needed me to help, so I jumped out of my blanket pallet on the floor and joined them. The last of the animals to be fed were the pigs. (The smell found me before we found the pigs!) We three—Uncle Andy, Grandpa, and I—stood on a rise above the pigs that were wallowing in their food and mud as dawn rose across the sky behind them. The scene was captivating.

Both Uncle Andy and Grandpa viewed the scene with one foot perched on the wooden fence rail and one hand cocked in a back pocket. I didn't have back pockets, and the lower rail was too high for my foot. So instead I shoved both hands into the back of my elastic-waist capris. I was mesmerized by the moment...until Grandpa snuck behind me, picked up a grasshopper, and suddenly dropped it in the gaping hole that my hands had made between my back and my pants. The grasshopper and I both danced wildly, accompanied by the men's good-natured laughter, which was soon joined by my own delighted screams.

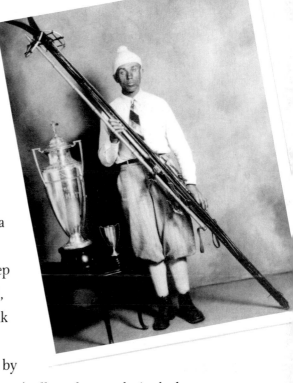

In light of such high jinks, it made sense that Grandma would be concerned when Grandpa disappeared from her sights. She would first step out on the porch and call, "Hen-REE!" and then walk the yard, trumpeting his absence to the neighbors by the same call. Grandpa wasn't allowed to smoke in the house, so he sometimes took off for the town park without telling anyone he was leaving. He would stroll for a while or sit on a bench and visit while he enjoyed a smoke.

Grandma would stew until he came home, and then she would gripe about his absence, for which he was properly contrite—but she rarely knew when to stop. She continued to question him about his activities until he became stone silent with her. After all, Grandpa had a strong notion as to what was right—so I shouldn't have been surprised when he came to my rescue one time.

I was about seven when, one night, I woke up screaming from a nightmare and a burning pain in my side. The doctor hovering over me in our little bedroom looked monstrous as he said I needed an appendectomy. I had recovered from a tonsillectomy only a month before and loathed going back into the hospital, but Grandpa met us in the parking lot and carried me through the doors. The comforting smell of his Old Spice was soon replaced with the vapor of ether.

During my recovery in the hospital, I spent most of my time alone, and the nurses were wickedly demanding. All of this broke my spirit, and I became quite despondent. One time a nurse came into my room and insisted that I drink a glass of grape juice. I didn't want grape juice, so I curled up into a ball for hours and just stared at the glass of juice.

When my family came to see me that evening, I told them of the abuse I suffered. The answer seemed obvious enough to most everyone: "Just drink your juice!" I told them that now it was warm and that I would surely throw up and rip out my stitches. Everyone laughed—everyone except Grandpa. In a more serious tone, he asked if he could talk to me alone. When the others were gone, Grandpa winked at me and quickly downed the juice.

This last incident was only one reason why I moved Grandpa and Grandma into my home some thirty years later. We had nine months together to talk and remember before he passed on, Grandma at his side. I like to think that he felt safe in our arms just as I once had in his. I will forever cherish memories of my time on earth with him, and I know that he watches over me even now. I can almost smell the Old Spice. ❋

*"I have a warm feeling after
playing with my grandchildren.
It's the liniment working."*

AUTHOR UNKNOWN

White-Glove Service

LAUREL SEILER BRUNVOLL

After walking the long stretch of corridor, my husband Steve and I finally reached the elevator. Our two sons, Josh and Mike, always in a constant race with one another, were already jockeying for button-pushing position.

"My turn!" quipped five-year-old Mike, who pushed his back sideways to Josh as he tried to monopolize the panel.

"No, I get to do it," Josh said with the authority of an older brother.

"You can take turns," my husband sighed. "One of you pushes it on the way up, and the other gets to do it on the way down."

That settled, we stepped in and waited for the slow-moving elevator to reach the fourth floor. When the door opened, Josh and Mike jumped out and peered down the right side of the hallway looking for Pop-Pop.

"Josh and Mike, here I am!" a voice called out from our left.

The boys turned and ran toward the familiar sound of their great-grandfather, whose huge grin greeted them. He reached out his arms and pulled them in on either side of him in a tight hug. "Pop-Pop, you're strong!" shouted Mike.

It was easy to see the effects of that compliment. Pop-Pop immediately looked more relaxed and happy, not quite so embarrassed of his new mode of getting around.

Pop-Pop was only recently confined to a wheelchair and missed not being able to interact with his grandchildren and great-grandchildren in the same ways as before. His fierce independence had kept him living on his own, driving a car, mowing the lawn, and raking leaves until he was ninety-one years old.

His strength, agility, and mental acumen were still very evident at age ninety-two, despite losing the ability to walk. Josh and Mike loved coming to visit Pop-Pop at the nursing home in Brooklyn, New York. Sometimes we would even stay and eat dinner with him and the other residents. Josh and Mike never complained about the food or the many requests for people to hold their hands, hug them, and simply admire their youthfulness.

"Who wants ice cream?" Pop-Pop asked the boys. He didn't have to ask twice before the boys started pushing his wheelchair toward the lounge area.

The ice cream social was just getting underway. Josh and Mike maneuvered the chair toward the far end of the table and then scooted two chairs up on each side of Pop-Pop. A dozen other seniors were sitting around, talking either to their neighbor or to themselves. Several seemed a bit sleepy for this afternoon activity.

One woman, who was sitting diagonally across from Pop-Pop and the boys, talked louder than anyone else.

An aide carefully placed bowls of vanilla ice cream topped with whipping cream and a token maraschino cherry in front of each person. After several moments of waiting, this lady frowned.

"Where's my ice cream? What is taking so long? How come no one is bringing me my ice cream?" she ranted.

Josh and Mike looked at Pop-Pop with concern. He winked his blue eyes at them and laughed. They smiled back.

"Hurry up!" she demanded.

Again, Josh and Mike looked worried, but Pop-Pop just gave them a hearty laugh. When they started to giggle, the older woman glared directly at Josh and Mike and yelled, "You'd better stop making that noise!"

An aide quickly brought her some ice cream, trying to soothe her agitation. The sundae worked its magic. She ate in silence while Josh and Mike devoured their large helpings of ice cream without ever looking up.

When Pop-Pop finished his share of sugar, he reached into his pocket and pulled out a white latex glove. "Watch this," he said, exhaling all his breath into it. The bloated glove grew and grew. Josh and Mike stared in fascination.

"Let me show you how I'd milk a cow when I was a boy," shared Pop-Pop. He held the end shut with one hand and used the other to demonstrate the milking action on one of the fingers. Pop-Pop grew up on a farm in southern Norway. As the second oldest of eight children, he inherited the responsibility for taking care of the animals since his father died when he was only eleven years old. He was well accustomed to this daily ritual.

Pop-Pop then poked the thumb of the glove in.

Boing! It popped back out!

All three of them laughed.

Josh took a turn at poking the thumb in.

Boing! It popped back out!

More laughter.

Mike took a turn at poking the thumb in.

Boing! It popped back out!

They could no longer stop laughing. Just at that moment, Pop-Pop let go of the glove. It made a quiet whooshing sound and flew in a circle above their heads. After a quick flip and turn, it took a sharp dive and landed...

Smack on top of the grumpy lady's chest!

None of us was able to hide our laughter as we made the decision to leave quickly. Pop-Pop and the boys relived the glove's antics over and over. Later, as we drove home Josh and Mike asked in unison, "Mom and Dad, when can we come visit Pop-Pop again?" ❊

"**I was born at night, but it wasn't last night!**"

"*When you have a grandchild,*
you have two children."

JEWISH PROVERB

Pépère's Habit

PHYLLIS MAY CARON GAGNON

One particular Thanksgiving will always stand out in my memory of family holiday celebrations. My father enjoyed cooking for these large family gatherings that were part of his heritage. He made the main meal while Mummy baked the traditional sixteen pies.

Arriving first, my grandfather Pépère emerged from his shiny, dark-green Buick sedan. Pépère loved nothing better than an audience. As family members of all ages arrived, the old man found himself surrounded by an adoring crowd.

This particular Thanksgiving, however, I noticed Mummy nervously watching him out of the corner of her eye.

"Raym, watch your father," she reminded Daddy.

Watch Pépère? Why? I wondered. I knew my handsome French-Canadian grandfather wore a glass eye. Was it giving him trouble today? Mummy had often told me how her carpenter father-in-law had lost his eye when a nail he was hammering flew back at him.

As Pépère winked his approval of Daddy's generously laden table, I silently scrutinized which one was the glass eye. It was impossible to tell. Both were a deep, shining blue.

Clean shaven with neatly combed snow-white hair, Pépère sat tall and straight in his gray suit, white shirt, and striped tie. *Pépère looks so handsome*, I thought. The revered patriarch held the seat of honor at the head of the table. I noticed that his broad smile did not betray the fact that he wore false teeth. Obviously relishing the presence of each member of his large family, he spoke half French, half English to those around him.

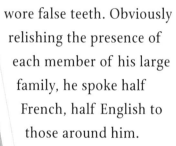

"Un autre morceau, s'il vous plaît," he was saying as Aunt Val heaped another slice of white meat on his plate. I calmed myself as I decided that Pépère was fine. Throughout the feast the old man told one silly story after another, all with a straight face.

"So when the guy wouldn't leave, I set my alarm in front of him.... The next morning I found him sound asleep at my kitchen table!"

Everyone laughed. By now Mummy appeared relaxed as she enjoyed her father-in-law's jovial tales. At last the plates were cleared.

"Time for Millie's pies!" Uncle Nellie declared.

But before they could be set out, I noticed a twinkle in Pépère's eye. Then the twinkle grew into a gleam. I now realized which one was the glass eye. Quietly my grandfather excused himself from the table.

No sooner had Pépère stepped out of the room than he reappeared, transformed into a grotesque figure. I saw my mother's features tighten as her eyes closed in horror.

"Raym! Raym!" she called to my father.

Twelve cousins, two uncles, three aunts, my parents, my sister, and a cat sat transfixed in amazement. There, groping through the kitchen in a gray suit, white shirt, and striped tie was a one-eyed creature with wild, mussed up white hair! The toothless intruder stumbled to the table and bumped my sister Leslie. Poor little thing shrieked and began to cry.

Across the table my older cousins Norm and Claire seemed to smirk behind their hands as they whispered to each other. Now the monster grabbed the napkin from my hand. Raving in half French, half English, it shouted at me, "Avez-vous encore du turkey?" and "Où sont les pies?"

The monster bumbled its way to the head of the table and plopped itself down—right in Pépère's seat! Screams from the girls and shouts from the boys combined with Mummy's pleas.

"Raym, Raym, stop him now!" she implored.

I joined my mother in loudly begging, "Help, help! Daddy, get him!"

I was dismayed and confused. Did my father think this was funny? Was he trying to hide a smile? My mother sternly indicated that the charade had gone on long enough. She demanded the creature disappear now! At last Daddy began to address the monster in French: "Pa, c'est assez, s'il vous plaît."

A moment later, as if on cue, Pépère reappeared, dressed in the same familiar gray suit, and he calmly sat down in the chair.

"Did I miss anything?" he asked with a straight face. ❋

"If it ain't broke, don't fix it!"

"I like to do nice things for my grandchildren—like buy them those toys I've always wanted to play with."

GENE PERRET

With a Whistle and a Wink

ANDREW HINKLE, AS TOLD TO CYNTHIA HINKLE

During my summer visits to his home, I always admired Grandfather Clifford's quirky resourcefulness. So, when our family arrived, I often headed for the basement. This was Grandpa's domain—his organized tool wonderland, where handmade toys and play equipment begged for my attention.

"Grandpa! Grandpa!" I yelled up the stairs.

My grandparents rushed down to me. "Are you all right, son?" they asked.

"I'm fine. Could I play outside on the putt-putt? Please, Gramps, may I?"

"Sure," he said. "I'll help you carry it to the garage for a gasoline fill-up."

"Cliff," Grandma protested. "That go-cart of yours has been idle for years."

"I lubricated it and gave it a thorough check this morning," he replied. "Now all we need to do is to conduct extensive test-drives on the road. Andy, would you like to be the first test-driver?"

"Oh yes!" I answered.

Grandpa Clifford grinned as Grandma shook her head and sighed.

Grandfather had built the putt-putt for his kids with a wooden box, belts, wheels, and an old Maytag washer engine. Of course, he had to rev down the mighty engine. But with a full tank of gas, that little putt-putt could drive an incredible two miles—on a dead-end street!

The summer after my second grade, Grandpa started tinkering on another of his inventions—the Vibra-Magic Color-Changing Wheel—that was based on a toy he once had. It began as a wooden stick with a propeller and morphed into a T-stick with two propellers. One summer it had five spinning disks of different colors. At first, this new toy had me scratching my crew-cut head. I could get it to spin, but only Grandpa knew the magic way to reverse the direction of the spin.

I remember him sitting at his workbench as he showed me new notches on a clear plastic rod under the glow of an incandescent light. Beside him were plastic disks, each with a hole in the center. He cut the outer edges into the shape of windmill paddles.

"Now, son, I'm going to bolt these wheels onto the end of this plastic shaft."

"Red, blue, and yellow," I said, now a perky nine-year old. "They're the primary colors."

"That's right, Andy. God's basic spectrum. Depending on the placement of each disk or wheel, you can blend the colors into secondary and tertiary colors. I'll put yellow up front of the red, like that. Now when you rub a coin on the notches, the wheels spin, and—"

"You get orange!" I shouted. "The yellow and blue wheels blend into green. The red and blue make purple. That's what you showed me last year, right?"

Through black-rimmed glasses, his eyes blinked a yes. "And we can spin red violet, blue violet, and so forth," he added.

"But, Gramps, does this new Vibra-Magic Color-Changing Wheel reverse its spin all by itself?"

Grandpa rubbed the coin against the notches in a back-and-forth rhythm. I fixed my eyes on the trio of wheels, and the spin of colors set me into a hypnotic trance. Grandpa whistled as the disks slowed and then started turning in the other direction.

"How's your whistle coming, son?" he asked.

Not breaking my stare, I answered, "Okay."

Grandpa had taught all his children how to whistle, down to the third generation. I don't recall the lessons, but I have a photograph of my son as a toddler astride his great-grandpa's knee, ready to purse his lips into a note.

"Well, now, Andy, let's hear that whistle. See if your whistle can make the Vibra-Magic Color-Changing Wheel whirl the other direction while I keep it running."

Slightly tone-deaf, I whistled as best as I could. I whistled repeatedly. Those wheels would not reverse. Then Grandpa gave me whistling pointers, plus a lesson in the Hinkle wink.

"Son," he said, "try spinning the wheel while you whistle."

Grandpa Clifford directed my hand across the notches. But, try as I might and in every tone I could hear and not hear, I couldn't alter the spin's direction with my whistles.

"I give up," I said, handing the toy back to him.

Rubbing the notches, my grandfather finally revealed the twofold secret solution to the problem. "One, the vibrations dampen and the wheels shift directions—but only at the pitch of my whistle. Number two, it's critical whose hand rubs across the rod."

I glanced up in time to see Grandpa Clifford do the wink. I'm sure he did that exact wink after his rubber worm popped from a folded, single-dollar tip to a waitress whose service lacked. And he winked that same way after his boss opened his buzzing rubber-band envelope on April Fools' Day. That wink began with a poker face, but the single-eyed blink was always followed by an all-knowing grin.

I stopped staring at the wheels and instead focused on the rod and Grandpa's sleight of hand on the coin. Grinning, I winked back.

Now, some forty years later, that Vibra-Magic Color-Changing Wheel sits in my basement near some engineering textbooks. Grandfather Clifford must wink from heaven whenever I demonstrate the magic wheel for my kids or anyone else. Naturally, I insist that only my whistle and only in my capable hands can those three wheels do a U-turn.

My kids groan and give me the wink. ❄

"Age is an issue of mind over matter.
If you don't mind, it doesn't matter."

MARK TWAIN

"Hold That Spot!"

SHERYL CAISSIE

Grandpa Louie. That's what we called him. His name was Louis Kasten. A Jewish immigrant from Poland, he came to the United States through Ellis Island and raised his family in Brooklyn, New York. Though soft-spoken and gentle, he had what we call *chutzpah*—a Yiddish word akin to our saying, "He's got a lot of nerve!" I didn't know my grandpa very well, but what memories I have of him melt my heart.

In the early part of my life, we lived close to my grandparents, and I saw them quite often. But when I was six years old, my family moved to Massachusetts. Our visits with Grandpa Louie and Grandma Hannah became much less frequent. We saw them about twice a year. They would come to the "country" each summer, and we would go to the city once a year to visit them. And those trips to Brooklyn were always memorable.

Grandma Hannah was a phenomenal baker. I remember sitting around Grandma and Grandpa's kitchen table with my cousins and siblings, eating cookie after cookie after cookie. No one made cookies like my grandmother. And the little paunch on Grandpa suggested that he enjoyed her baking too!

Grandpa Louie never said much. He smiled. He chanted little tunes. Tunes I had never heard before. Little ditties with a Yiddish flair to them. That humming of his was his trademark! When we visited, Grandpa spent most of the time sitting in his harvest-gold reclining chair and watching the goings-on. That chair now sits in my basement.

At the time my grandparents purchased that new recliner, it was something to be proud of. Planted directly in front of the television, it was carefully covered in plastic—like all the furniture in my grandparents' house. Now, whenever I sit in that old, beat-up recliner, I think of my grandfather and how unassuming he seemed. Considering his quiet demeanor, I am still surprised when I recall the first time I realized what chutzpah Grandpa actually had!

Trying to find a parking space in Brooklyn is like trying to squeeze a camel through the eye of a needle! That's why, when we went on our annual trek to my grandparents' Brooklyn apartment, my dad's greatest concern was "Where will we find a parking space?!" But Grandpa Louie had it all under control. We always called him before we left the house so he'd know approximately when we would arrive. There were no cell phones for us to communicate en route, so he had to carefully predict our driving time, being sure to consider traffic backups and wrong turns when calculating our estimated time of arrival.

I vividly remember one visit in particular. We approached the street where Grandpa Louie lived. Both sides of the street were, as usual, packed with cars. Not a single empty spot in sight. But wait! There was a spot. There was no car in that spot, but...there was a little man standing squarely in it. There he was, "parked" on the roadside as if he himself were a car! From a distance, we saw him boldly waving cars away as they tried to pull into the spot. Drivers honked.  They sneered. *What a lunatic!* we thought as we drove up closer. *Who would do such a thing?*

As we approached that spot, we saw none other than our dear grandpa Louie, directing us into the parking space. He had been standing out there, not concerned about what people would think of him, but kindly wanting to be sure we had a place to park after our long drive into the city.

As I stand up and walk away from the recliner, I turn back to look at it. That chair symbolically has its own parking spot in our cellar, reminding me of a diminutive man with a reserved nature, a big heart, and the chutzpah of one with the conviction and audacity to stand in the middle of Brooklyn and say, "I've got to hold that spot!" ❋

It hurts to be stupid.

*"The old are the precious gem
in the center of the household."*

CHINESE PROVERB

Bread Dough and Boots

NANCY B. KENNEDY

N o, stop!"

"Don't do it, Grandpa!"

"Grandma, make him stop!"

The three of us sisters, little girls at the time, huddled around a mixing bowl on the floor of our grandparents' kitchen, protecting its precious contents with our small bodies. We were visiting our grandparents in western Pennsylvania, and Grandma Boyd had moved her bread-making operation to the floor, so we could safely help without teetering on chairs at the counter.

When it came time to punch down the dough, Grandpa would appear at the kitchen door in his steel-toed work boots. Grandpa was a quiet man, a farmer much of his life and later the owner of a hardware store. He didn't say much, but at moments like this his eyes would shine with a glint of sly humor.

Taking deliberate steps, he advanced toward us and at last he raised his foot over the bowl. Slowly, he lowered his foot, his massive boot coming ever closer to the yeasty bubble. The three of us shrieked, and we made quite a racket. Girls are good at that. Grandma shook her finger and tut-tutted crossly at Grandpa, frowning at her beloved husband.

"Now, Basil, don't you dare!" she scolded.

Finally, at the last moment, Grandpa relented. He dropped his foot back on the floor and went silently on his way. Our shrieks changed to giggles then, and we returned to our bread making.

I'm grateful for this memory of my grandfather because, as a young child, I was sometimes afraid of him.

Grandpa Boyd was tall and austere, the kind of stern forebearer often pictured in old family photographs. By the time I knew him, he was diabetic and had to eat sparingly from my grandmother's bountiful table. His skin was pale and thinly stretched over his gaunt frame. But most fearful for me—as it would be for almost any child, I would think—was that his right hand was locked into an immobile claw. I could barely bring myself to look at his hand, it scared me so, and I shrank from its touch.

You see, my grandfather grew up on a farm, my great-grandfather Nathan's farm in Stoneboro, Pennsylvania, and even as a young child, he helped with the farmwork. One day in 1914, when he was fourteen years old, he was out driving the farm's horse-drawn hay mower. The hay was heavy and had clogged up the cutting blades. He stopped to clear them by hand, just as someone today might clear a rake jammed with leaves. At that moment, something startled the horses—whether a sight or a sound, no one can say. They jumped, pulling the mower with them, and the blades sliced through my grandfather's hand, almost severing it entirely.

Surgery saved my grandfather's hand, but the tendons couldn't be reattached. As his hand healed, his fingers closed inward. But he was determined not to let his handicap hinder him. He taught himself to write again, and he even went back to driving the horses, wrapping the reins around his disabled hand. He took over his father's farm, running it until 1938 when his health forced him to abandon it in favor of the hardware business.

Even today, so many years later, I can picture that farm and especially my grandparents' house: their small white house sat at the top of a rise just beyond the Wesleyan Methodist camp-meeting ground. I can so effortlessly put myself in those rooms

again, into that cozy kitchen where we made bread. I remember
once hiding in a hallway closet and weeping in sorrow because
our parents were leaving us there for a week. And I remember,
as a ten-year-old, sitting by the backdoor on the day of my
grandfather's funeral. I was playing with the snapdragons,
pinching the folds of the flowers into tiny mouths. I remember
later visiting my grandmother in another house in town, the
one she shared with her sister until her death eight years after
her husband's death.

Oh, how I would love to spend a week with my grandparents
now! My heart aches with a deep longing for that reunion. One
day it will happen, and when in heaven it does, I will finally let
myself be enfolded in my grandfather's embrace, completed, as it
will be, with a new hand. But even so, in that very moment, I
think I might still keep an eye out for Grandpa's foot. ❋

"I'm no spring chicken you know."

"Grandchildren: the only people who can get more out of you than the IRS."

GENE PERRET

Playing Cards

STEPHANIE SNYDER RICCI

My grandfather is a fine, upstanding citizen who loves his family, his church, and his country, all unconditionally. He supported his six children by working two jobs, yet all of them remember that he always had time for throwing a baseball, attending their games and concerts, or going out for ice cream. We grandchildren remember growing up with Grandpa as he continues the same traditions with his great-grandchildren now.

In particular, he loves to teach children card games, probably because he truly enjoys the actual playing and could not care less about the outcome. I loved to sit down and play with him, but I have the sort of brain that promptly forgets the rules of most games soon after I stop playing them. In my youngest brother, however, my grandfather found a kindred spirit.

From the time he was a preschooler, Matt had a head for games. He learned his numbers from playing cards; he remembered even the most obscure rules; and he posed a challenge to adults with his knack for understanding and employing strategy. Grandpa was a great teacher, who gracefully walked the line between instructor and fellow competitor.

He expected fair play from everyone, and he allowed us all to learn the game by respecting our intelligence and letting us make mistakes. There was no artificial self-esteem boosting and no letting us win by intentionally playing poorly. Nothing made Grandpa's eyes twinkle more than a grandchild beating him, fair and square. Matt and my grandfather quickly progressed from kid-friendly games like War and Go Fish to cribbage and various forms of poker.

One day, my mother was volunteering in Matt's kindergarten class. Working with a group of children, one that did not include my brother, she was only peripherally aware of what he was doing nearby with another group. She overheard another student ask, "Matt, what did you say this game was called?"

"Five-card stud," answered my five-year-old brother.

Cringing from embarrassment and certain that her good reputation had been destroyed, my mother intervened and redirected the students—who I'm sure were disappointed that their gambling tutorial had been interrupted. Later she had a talk with Matt about why poker was not really appropriate for school.

And later on she called my grandfather to tell him about the incident. Both of them laughed the way adults laugh at precocious children—when out of their hearing, with genuine amusement, and a little sheepish that they are at the root of it all.

My grandfather is eighty-nine years old and very pleased that my four-year-old daughter loves to play Go Fish with him. I will be having the poker talk with her before she goes off to kindergarten. ❄

"Don't eat yellow snow."

"As you are at seven, so you are at seventy."

JEWISH PROVERB

Round and Round

BY LAUREL SEILER BRUNVOLL

I walked into my grandfather's garage from the backyard. "It's hanging on the left wall, near the window," he shouted in his crisp, midwestern accent. "Bring some of those little nails on the bench too, please. They're in a red box."

He was on a mission to fix the squirrel feeder he had recently built. Gray squirrels came from miles around to ride the brightly colored Ferris wheel on his manicured lawn. Each wooden bucket was freshly painted in a different color and dutifully filled with sunflower seeds every morning. Grandpa would sit at the dining room table, gaze out the back window, and wait for a show—sometimes for hours.

He might see a few leaves rustle gently against the oak tree's branches that swayed above the three-foot-high wooden structure. The six colored baskets would rock ever so slightly in the Wisconsin summer air that was neither cold nor hot.

Finally, Grandpa's patience would be rewarded: a large group of squirrels started playing tag at the base of a large tree. They took turns chasing one another across the cut grass, under bushes, through neat rows of flowers, and up and down tree trunks. Back and forth they raced around the yard and took turns being "it."

After several minutes, a handful of energetic critters scrambled up a tree and did a tightrope act on fast-forward mode. They didn't even wait for a dramatic musical introduction or nets to be put in place. They simply scurried and jumped from branch to branch, stopping briefly to regain footholds before setting their sights on the next high spot. Once in a while, a squirrel would slip, lose its grasp, and catch itself before falling.

In the center ring sat the famous Ferris wheel—the squirrels' favorite destination. Drawn by food or possibly adrenalin rushes from the ride, several squirrels approached it. My grandpa leaned forward in his chair and grabbed a pair of black binoculars. He forgot all about his cup of coffee and glass of orange juice, squeezed only an hour before by my grandmother.

The least timid squirrel in the crowd hopped into a blue basket and hung on as it started rocking. At the same time, the whole wheel rotated counterclockwise. The squirrel then leaped straight up and landed in the next basket, causing the wheel to move faster. Soon another squirrel jumped in. The momentum of the second rider's weight pushed the first squirrel up to the crest before it began a rapid descent on the other side.

Unfortunately, the squirrel wasn't wearing a seatbelt and couldn't handle the g-forces. It was flung off just before completing the circular route. This fun continued for quite some time as more squirrels joined in, and my grandpa would never leave his seat until things quieted down.

Shortly before our family's visit, however, two rather large squirrels got on the Ferris wheel at the same time and broke it. Maybe it spun too fast and stressed the supports. (By the way, I believe I can pinpoint exactly when and where those rodents started gaining their extra pounds.)

So, following instructions, I quickly reached up and grabbed a hammer. It looked the perfect size for hammering in small-sized nails. Even as a nine-year-old I noticed how neatly Grandpa's tools hung on the pegboards. He even knew where the hammer was without having to come with  me to find it, I remember thinking. Rakes, shovels, and brooms all stood at attention at the perimeter while saws lay quietly in a custom-built box. I wondered why our own garage didn't look like this.

Grandpa efficiently nailed the squirrel feeder back together, taking time to fill each colored bin with a handful of seeds. Mission accomplished, it was time for him to head out with the grandkids. Every day during our visits, he took my sister Becky and me to a playground and then to the library. We always went to a different playground around the city and reveled in the uniqueness of each one. He was the only adult who ever really played with me. He ran and jumped and pushed our swings, and our games of chase lasted as long as we could last.

Then, breathless, we would pile back into his always-vacuumed car and drive to a local library. He proudly held out his library card to get books checked out for us. Curious George was always among our choices.

I can't remember how old I was when I started doing the reading. Usually grandfathers read to their grandchildren, but he always asked us to read to him. He was a great listener even as I stumbled over words and guessed at pronunciation. He didn't correct me, and he never seemed bored. (I found out many years later he had only an eighth-grade education and was a bit self-conscious about reading aloud.)

As much as I loved Curious George stories, though, I loved listening to my grandpa's made-up bedtime stories more. When we were carefully tucked under the sheets and blankets, his voice became almost menacing as he told the monster part of the story. Then he would shake the bed as my sister and I squealed with pretend terror.

It only took a few minutes of screaming before we heard a yell. "George, for gosh sakes, get up here now and let those kids get to sleep," my grandmother would holler down the stairs. Even though he looked like he'd been caught, he'd continue for a tad bit longer and give us a special wink.

In the morning, my sister and I raced upstairs to eat breakfast. I can still picture Grandpa by the window, wearing worn leather slippers and a faded blue-plaid flannel shirt with khaki pants. He was already there waiting for us.

Apparently, we had missed some early-morning antics, because three squirrels were in a football huddle in front of the Ferris wheel. Perfectly poised in a sitting-up position, each squirrel grasped a single sunflower seed in its tiny paws. They alternately bit, chewed, and spit out shells. When they finished gorging themselves, all three turned their heads and flashed their wispy tails. They loved my grandpa almost as much as I did. ❋

"To forget one's ancestors is to be a brook without a source, a tree without a root."

CHINESE PROVERB

Walk on Water

LARRY HARRIS

When I was twelve years old, I thought my grandfather could walk on water. That is, until I found out his secret.

It was an unspoken tradition that my cousin Donnie and I would go fishing with Papa Davis whenever we visited his home in Hohenwald, Tennessee. We often met there for the weekend. Sometimes we rode down with our families; sometimes I would take a bus from Nashville. No matter how we arrived, it was always with great anticipation of fishing on the Buffalo River.

My grandfather had been a guide on the Buffalo before his stroke, and he knew everything there was to know about that area. Donnie and I enjoyed hearing his stories as much as we enjoyed fishing. Unlike school mornings at home, we jumped out of bed on Saturday mornings in Hohenwald.

"Come on, Papa. Let's go!" we urged.

"Grab your poles, boys. Get in the car."

We loaded our cane poles and a bucket of minnows into the trunk of Papa's '53 Chevy Bel Air and took off. After stopping to pick up a lunch of bologna and white cheese at the local grocery, we left town on the same blacktop we took to church on Sunday mornings. However, when we reached the turnoff to Oak Grove Methodist Church, where Papa was music minister, we turned in the opposite direction onto a chert road, a combination of dirt and gravel. A whirlwind of dust followed us all the way to the river!

As soon as we arrived at the fishing hole, Papa parked under the shade of nearby oak trees and unpacked the car. Donnie and I immediately ran to the river. We carefully maneuvered down the slippery bank, laughing and sliding into the water.

A few feet from the bank we usually stood waist deep. That is, until we slipped and fell—and we inevitably fell! The rock bottom of the Buffalo was slick and slimy from algae and other underwater growth. It was nearly impossible to stand up for any length of time on those slippery rocks—unless you were Harry Davis, our grandpa. My cousin and I were always amazed at the way Papa skillfully navigated that river bottom. When we asked him how he did it, he just smiled.

Then, at the end of one of our fishing trips, we prepared to return home for supper. Donnie and I were especially tired, so we followed Papa to the car instead of lagging behind for one last gaze at the river. As I watched Papa take off his wet shoes and put them in the trunk, I couldn't believe my eyes!

They were golf shoes! Papa's secret to walking along the
Buffalo bottoms was cleats!

    After that, I loved to tease Papa about the secret he had kept
from us. But the truth is, he taught me a lot about life: Things are
not always what they appear.... It's best to be prepared before you
set out upon the treacherous rocks of life.... And grandkids
should always believe their grandfathers walk on water. ✻

Acknowledgments

Thank you to my literary agent Bill Jensen... for your friendship, encouragement, and help. I'm so glad we get to work together again.

Thank you to my editor Lisa Stilwell... for your guidance, suggestions, and hard work. Your editing touch made a difference.

Thank you to all my contributing writers... for sharing your wonderful grandparent stories. I'm hopeful these accounts will inspire others to preserve and treasure their own family memories.

Thank you to my incredible family—to my loving husband, Steve, and to my awesome, fun-loving sons, Josh and Mike. Your support and encouragement mean more than you'll ever know. I love you!

Most of all, thank You, God, for being an ever-constant presence in my life. I'm hopeful that this book will bring happiness and joy to families everywhere.

If you enjoyed this book, you'll also enjoy

*All My Good Habits
I Learned from Grandma*